Country Mosaics for Scrollers and Crafters

by Frank Droege

Fox
Chapel Publishing Co. Inc.

1970 Broad Street • East Petersburg, PA 17520 • www.foxchapelpublishing.com

Country Mosaics for Scrollers & Crafters is a brand new work, first published in 2003 by Fox Chapel Publishing Company, Inc. The patterns contained herein are copyrighted by the author. Artists purchasing this book have permission to make up to three photocopies of each individual pattern for personal use only. The patterns themselves are not to be duplicated for resale or distribution under any circumstances.

Publisher:	Alan Giagnocavo
Editor:	Ayleen Stellhorn
Layout and Design:	Linda L. Eberly
Cover Design:	David Marty
Interior Photography:	Harry Troutman

ISBN 1-56523-179-1
Library of Congress Preassigned Card Number: 2002114655

To order your copy of this book,
please send check or money order for the cover price
plus $3.00 shipping to:

Fox Books
1970 Broad Street
East Petersburg, PA 17520

Or visit us on the web at *www.foxchapelpublishing.com*

Printed in China
10 9 8 7 6 5 4 3 2 1

Table of Contents

About the Author

Designing scroll saw mosaic patterns and pieces can be described as a passionate pastime for Frank Droege. Frank's first love is painting. Over the years, he has won numerous awards as a traditional painter. Frank studied under George Vail from the Haddonfield Art League and under Max Gottlieb at the Fleisher Art Memorial in Philadelphia, Pennsylvania. He currently paints miniature art and has recently become an award-winning artist in the field. Frank lives in Voorhees, New Jersey, with his wife and daughters. Inquiries about his artwork can be addressed directly to Frank at 306 Kresson-Gibbsboro Road, Voorhees, NJ 08043.

Editor's Note: While the patterns in this book were specifically designed for the scroll saw, we believe that Frank's patterns can easily be applied to other handcrafts that use segmented designs. Quilting, rug hooking, needlepoint, embroidery, stained glass, paper piecing and tole painting are just a few suggestions.

Introduction

The country-themed patterns in this book were inspired by the Pennsylvania German traditions that are so prominent in the countryside around the author's home. Their symbols of peace, long life and prosperity can be seen on the hex signs that hang on their barns, on the house blessings that grace their homes, and on the quilts and furniture that they use and sell.

Noting the clean lines and bright colors of these designs, the author has translated these symbols into attractive segmentation patterns. Many of the symbols have unique meanings, which, when combined, create a special message for the owner.

Once cut, painted and assembled following basic segmentation techniques, the resulting pieces become excellent gifts and beautiful keepsakes.

STEP 1: Cut two boards, each measuring ¼" larger than the pattern you intend to scroll.

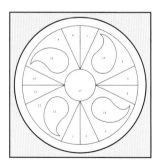

STEP 2: Glue the pattern to the pattern board with a light coat of spray adhesive. Set the backer board aside. (You may want to add numbers to the pieces to make reassembling the patterns easier).

NOTE: The difficulty level of any of these pieces can be reduced by changing the lines to reduce the number of pieces to be cut.

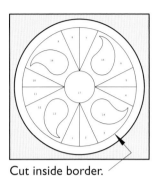

STEP 3: Cut the inside border of the pattern.

Cut inside border.

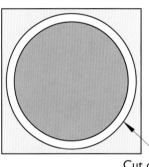

Cut outside of frame.

STEP 4: Remove the center piece and set it aside. Glue the pattern board to the backer board. Cut the outside of the frame.

STEP 5: Set the frame aside. Cut the pattern pieces. If you added numbers, transfer them to the back of the pieces.

STEP 6: Sand and paint the pieces. Using the numbers as a guide, glue the pieces into position inside the frame. Spray finish.

GOOD FORTUNE ROSETTE

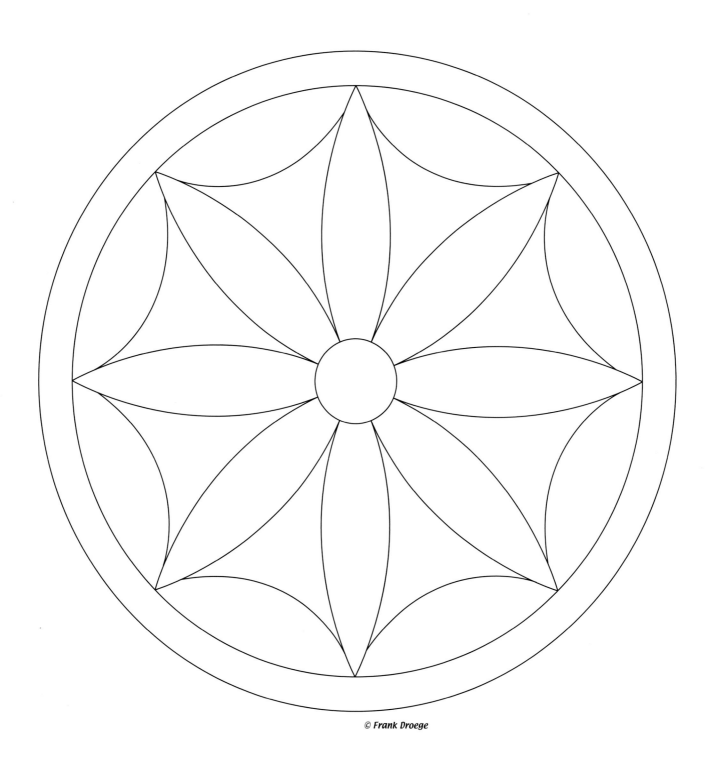

© Frank Droege

The rosette is the general symbol of good fortune. A simple rosette pattern such as this ensures overall good fortune for the owner.

Star rosette

© Frank Droege

 The star is a symbol of good luck. This simple star brings luck to its owner.

Water wheel

© Frank Droege

Water drops in an unending circle provide the owner of this sign with an abundance of water for his crops and gardens.

LUCKY AT LOVE

© Frank Droege

Hex Signs

The good luck of the star symbol combined with the circle of hearts grants the owner good luck in courting and marriage.

LUCK NEVER ENDING

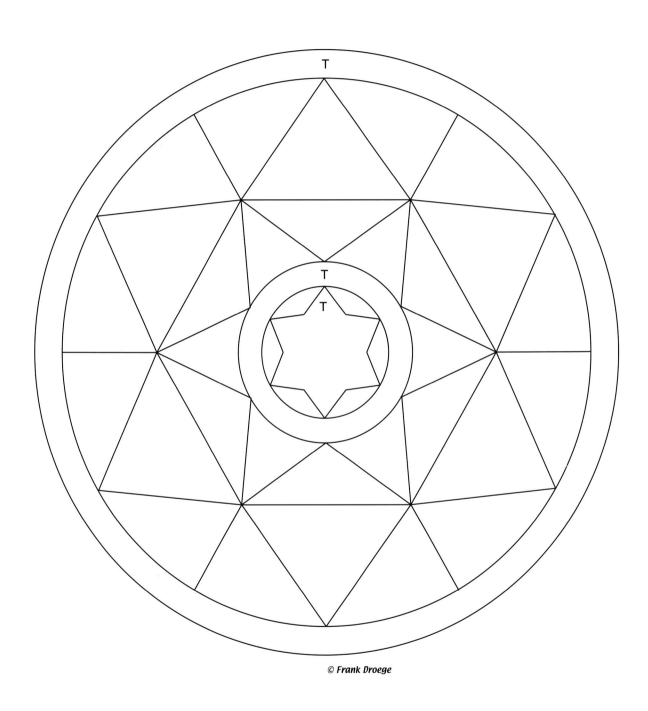

© Frank Droege

A repeating star pattern brings a never-ending cycle of growing luck and good fortune to the owner of this plaque.

LIGHT OF LIFE

© Frank Droege

Hex Signs

The eight-pointed star represents a stylized sun and blesses the owner of this plaque with the sun's warmth and light.

KALEIDOSCOPE OF LUCK

© Frank Droege

Another repeating star pattern promises luck and good fortune in any number of situations.

HAPPINESS AND GOOD FORTUNE

© Frank Droege

HAPPINESS AND GOOD FORTUNE

 The distelfink is a mystical bird. Its presence brings great happiness and good fortune to every occasion.

STRENGTH IN LOVE

© Frank Droege

The two-headed bird is a sign of strength. With the addition of an oversized heart at the bird's center, this design grants strength in love.

ORCHARD OF PLENTY

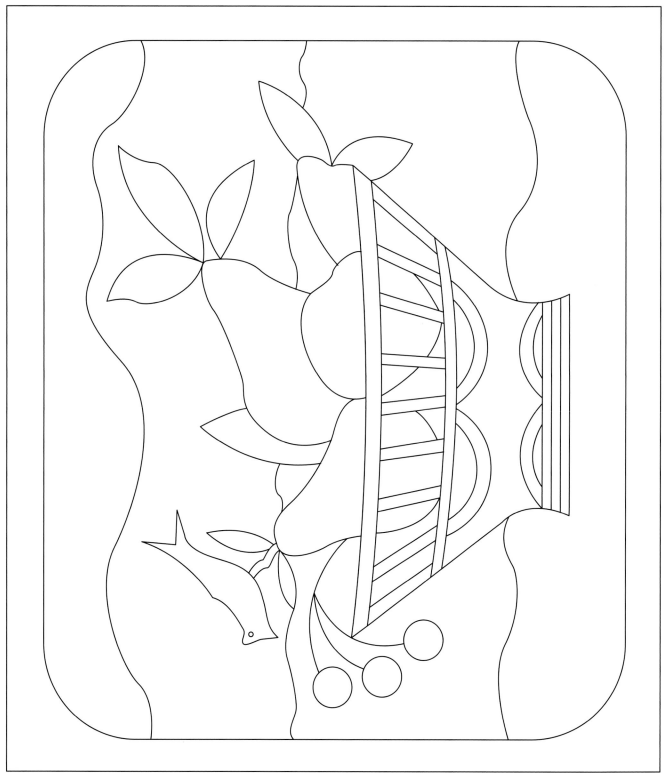

© Frank Droege

A basket filled with fruit from the orchards symbolizes a bountiful harvest.

BOUNTIFUL HARVEST

© Frank Droege

The cornucopia is a common symbol of bounty.
Here it is filled with orchard fruit.

Life's blessings

© Frank Droege

Fruit & Flowers

Green, growing plants represent life; three of anything represents faith. This design reminds the owner of his blessings in life.

TRINITY OF FAITH

© Frank Droege

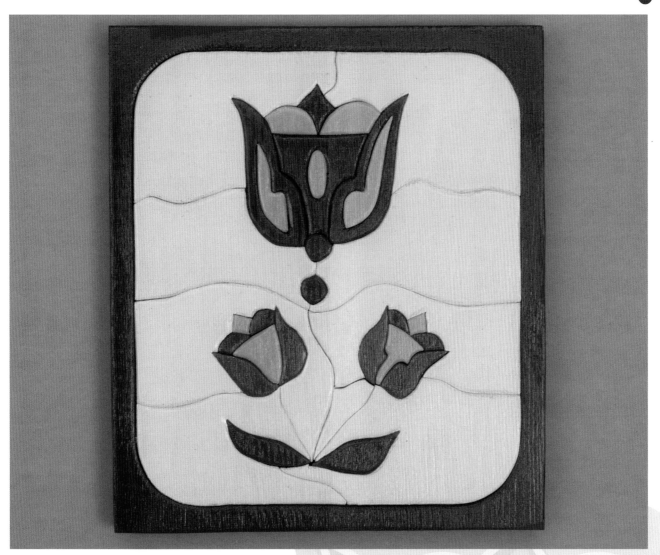

Tulips are a symbol of faith. Three tulips is generally understood to represent a religious or spiritual faith.

FAITHFUL BOUNTY

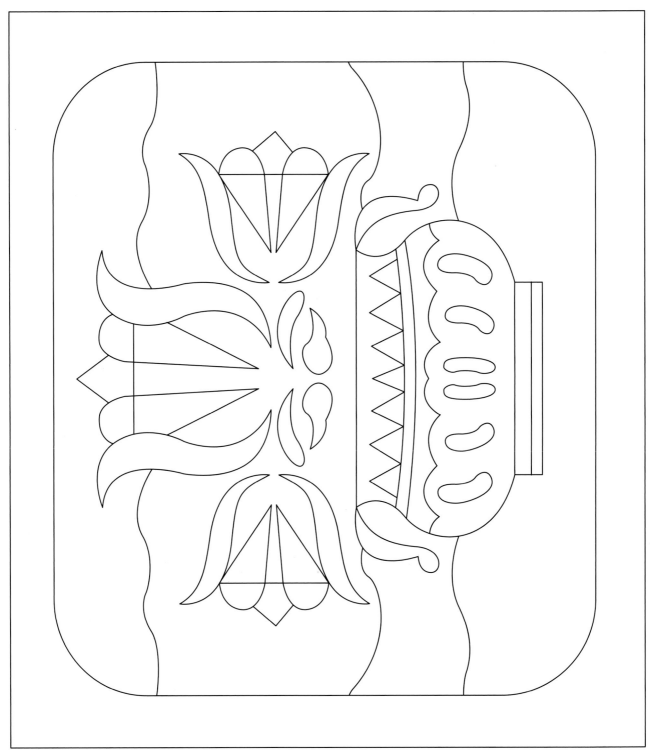

© Frank Droege

 Faith in life's bounty is represented by three tulips in a colorful bowl.

FLORAL DELIGHT

© Frank Droege

Plants represent life and growth. The addition of brightly colored flowers to the green stem symbolizes happiness throughout life.

Blooming love

© Frank Droege

The double heart represents two people joining in marriage. The scalloped edge grants smooth sailing in life.

Blossoming faith

© Frank Droege

Fruit & Flowers

Another marriage blessing, this design includes two hearts to symbolize the husband and wife plus the three tulips to represent faith.

Faith and love

© Frank Droege

"Have faith that love will prevail" is the message of this design. Love is represented by the heart; faith is represented by the three flowers.

LIFE'S BOUNTY

© Frank Droege

Greenery and growing plants symbolize life's bounty. The addition of the tulips reminds the owner to have faith in the bounty that life provides.

LIFE'S BEAUTY

© Frank Droege

A symbol of life's bounty, the greenery and growing plants in this design remind the owner to have faith in the beauty that surrounds him.

Growing in faith

© Frank Droege

"Small deeds yield great rewards" is the message behind this design. The grouping of three flowers reminds the owner to have faith in his actions.

THREE FLORALS

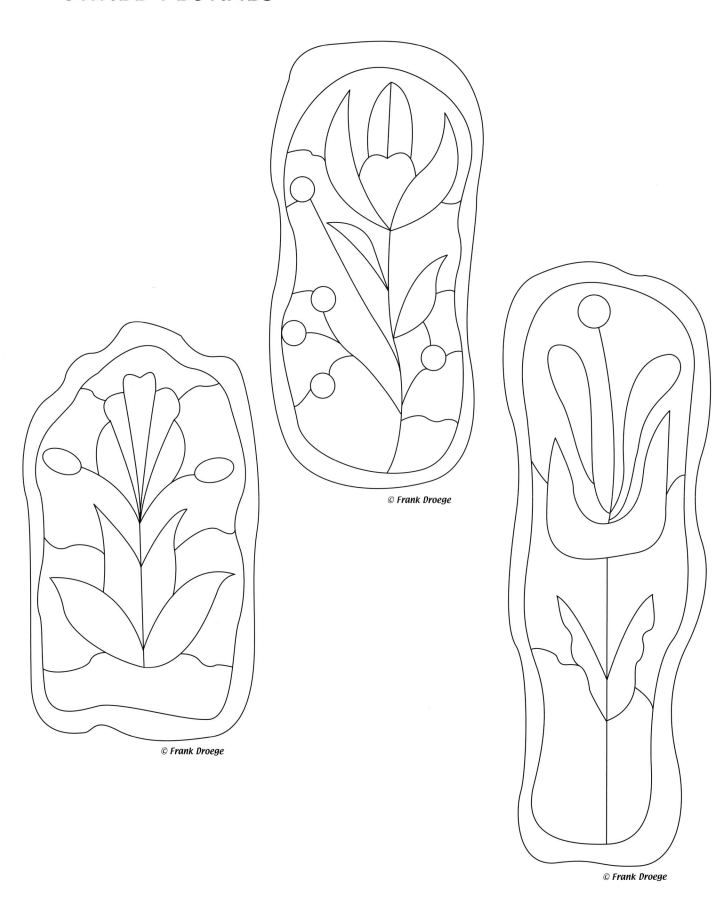

© Frank Droege

© Frank Droege

© Frank Droege

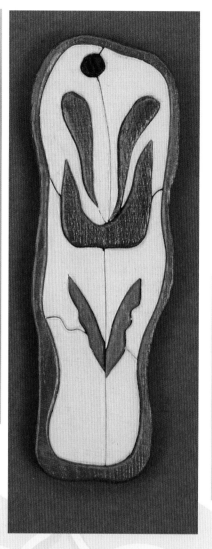

Fruit & Flowers

Flowers are an often repeated motif in country designs. These three floral designs can be made separately or as a group.

Faith's good fortune

© Frank Droege

*A tulip, symbolizing faith, is combined with
a rosette, symbolizing good fortune.*

BOUNTIFUL LOVE

© Frank Droege

The heart shape of this design represents love. The growing tulips bless the owner with faith in a growing love.

Love and faith enduring

© Frank Droege

Green leaves and flowers combined with a heart remind the owner of the continuous growth of love and faith.

Fruit & Flowers

Best wishes

© Frank Droege

 A scalloped edge signifies smooth sailing through life's troubles.

Birds & Animals

CONTINUING LUCK

© Frank Droege

Stars for luck combined with a bounding deer represent luck that continues throughout the owner's life.

Marriage blessing

© Frank Droege

 This marriage blessing incorporates doves, which symbolize peace, and a double heart to represent the bride and groom.

Birds & Animals

Beauty abounds

© Frank Droege

A bird surrounded by flowers reminds the owner to take notice of the beauty of life that surrounds him.

Seeds of life

© Frank Droege

Flowing greenery reminds the owner that seeds of life can grow despite many situations.

LIFE'S TREASURES

© Frank Droege

The three tulips of faith combined with a bird remind the owner to search for the hidden treasures that are not always apparent in life.

Birds & Animals

LIFE'S JOURNEY

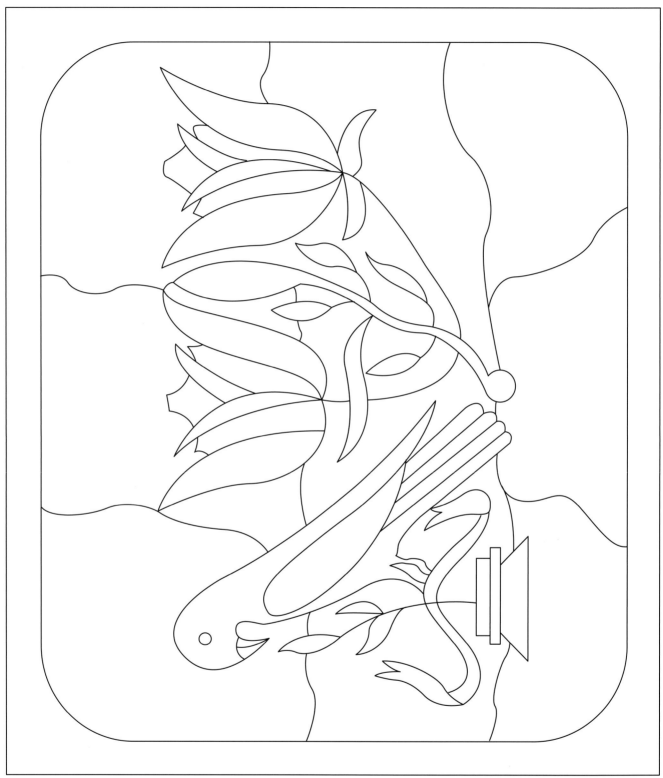

© Frank Droege

This design affords the owner with a blessing of faith and guidance as he travels through life's pleasures and disappointments.

Birds & Animals

ENCHANTED SUMMER

© Frank Droege

Growth, suggested by the green leaves, and beauty, suggested by the flower and the bird, are combined to wish the owner a pleasurable and profitable summer.

Birds & Animals